CW00670798

The Knowledge
book of

Notes & Quotes

Edited by Jon Connell

Illustrations
by Maddy Fletcher

First published in 2023 by
Connell Publishing
Spye Arch House
Spye Park
Lacock
Wiltshire
SN15 2PR

10 9 8 7 6 5 4 3 2 1

A CIP catalogue record for this book is available from the British Library.
ISBN 978-1-911187-96-7

Assistant Editors:
Paul Woodward & Iona Blayney

Printed in Great Britain

See our selection of literary and history guides at
www.connellguides.com

www.theknowledge.com

Contents

Introduction

What makes a good quote? In some cases, it's the literary equivalent of hitting a nail on the head. In others, it's a *bon mot* that just makes you laugh. Often good quotes are like flashes in the dark – they encapsulate truths we're vaguely aware of but somehow haven't or couldn't put into words. Or into words so well, or so succinctly, or elegantly, or amusingly. Sometimes, too, good quotes surprise us, even shock us, by taking a well-known conventional view and turning it on its head. Oscar Wilde is the master of this. I won't cite examples here but you'll find several in the pages that follow.

At any rate, that much overworked phrase "wit and wisdom" does the job best. When I started The Week one of my first decisions was to include such a column, and now, with The Knowledge, as regular readers will know, we include a quote every day. Often, though not always, these quotes are aimed to lift our spirits a little.

I've spent the last 30 years or so collecting quotes and in putting this collection together I've kept reminding myself of what George Orwell said of a fellow author: that he was "no more able to resist a quotation than some people are to refuse a drink".

Orwell's right, and it's the reason I'm allergic to dictionaries of quotations where you have to wade through endless *aperçus* and less-than-witty sayings from well-known people whose words have been immortalised solely because they're well known. So this particular collection is very personal, though many of the quotes, of course, have appeared in The Knowledge, and they've all been chosen purely on their own merits.

Just two practical points. I've laid this out in slightly arbitrary sections, to make it easier to read, or dip into, and I've been a little arbitrary in identifying sources. It's always a balance between assuming too much knowledge, and too little. In many cases I've just named the person quoted; in others I've been more descriptive. I hope the result won't send you rushing off too often to consult Google.

Finally, a word of thanks to all those who've helped me assemble these quotes, and in particular to the team at The Knowledge who did so much to make this collection possible: Michele Lavery, Harry Byford, Charlie Lyons, Jos Gogarty, Taz Chowdhury, and Christopher Fordham. Nor do I forget the shrewd counsel I've had from my long-suffering family – Alexandra, Ivar, Flora and Ciara – with the third of those, Flora, being part of both camps since she is also my trusty adviser on The Knowledge, and has been since those distant lockdown days when we first conceived it.

Jon Connell, November 2023

HOW TO
GET BY
IN LIFE

"Don't get so busy making
a living you forget to
make a life."

Dolly Parton

"We are what we pretend to be,
so we must be careful about
what we pretend to be."
Kurt Vonnegut

"Talk low, talk slow and don't say much."
John Wayne

"Never have a meeting on a Wednesday,
as it ruins both weekends."
Old adage

"Smile. Tomorrow will be worse."
**American engineer
Edward Murphy**

"The most certain sign of wisdom
is cheerfulness."
**French philosopher
Michel de Montaigne**

"Always fly first class. Or your children will."
Jeremy Clarkson

"Do the right thing. It will gratify some people and astonish the rest."
Mark Twain

"When choosing between two evils, I always pick the one I haven't tried before."
Mae West

"If at first you don't succeed, try, try again. Then quit. No use being a damn fool about it."
Comedian WC Fields

"Always be sincere, even if you don't mean it."
Harry Truman, US president 1945-53

"You mustn't wonder what is this person thinking about me, you must ask yourself, what am I thinking about them?"
Nigel Nicholson, recalling advice from Virginia Woolf

"The one thing I have learned over the years is the difference between taking one's work seriously and one's self seriously. The first is imperative and the second is disastrous."
Margot Fonteyn

"You only have to do a very few things right in your life, so long as you don't do too many things wrong."
Warren Buffet

"I was so horrified by what I read of the effects of smoking that I gave up reading."

Anonymous

Who needs advice?

"I always pass on good advice. It's the only thing to do with it. It is never of any use to oneself."
Oscar Wilde

"Use advisers carefully... Above all don't ask them for advice."
British businessman Hugh Osmond

"We are never so generous as when giving advice."
French writer François de La Rochefoucauld

"I have found the best way to give advice to your children is to find out what they want and then advise them to do it."
Harry Truman

"One should try everything once, except incest and folk dancing."
English composer Arnold Bax

"Never tell people how to do things. Tell them what to do and they will surprise you with their ingenuity."
US General George Patton

"The best way to cheer yourself is to try to cheer somebody else up."
Mark Twain

"Nothing gives one person so great an advantage over another, as to remain always cool and unruffled under all circumstances."
Thomas Jefferson, US president 1801-1809

"It's a funny thing about life; if you refuse to accept anything but the best, you very often get it."
W Somerset Maugham

"Do remember to place your candles in the fridge for two or three hours before use, or they could burn unevenly."
Guide for training navy cooks, quoted in The Guardian

"Never put off till tomorrow what you can do the day after tomorrow."
Mark Twain

"Never write when you can speak. Never speak when you can nod."
Legendary Boston politician Martin Lomasney

"If you always do what interests you,
at least one person is pleased."
Katharine Hepburn

"Several excuses are always less
convincing than one."
Aldous Huxley

"The minute you settle for less than you
deserve, you get even less than you
settled for."
**New York Times columnist
Maureen Dowd**

"Attention is the rarest and purest form of generosity."
French philosopher Simone Weil

"If you would stand well with a great mind, leave him with a favourable impression of yourself; if with a little mind, with a favourable impression of himself."
Samuel Taylor Coleridge

"Yield to temptation.
It may not pass your way again."
**Science fiction writer
Robert Heinlein**

The heights that great men reached and kept
Were not attained by sudden flight,
But they, while their companions slept,
Were toiling upward in the night.
**Longfellow, from *The Ladder of
St Augustine* (1858)**

"Sit as little as possible, and give no credence to any thought that was not born outdoors."
Nietzsche

"My grandmother told me to find something nice to say about everyone and say it."
Jilly Cooper

"Goodness you've done well,"
Mae West was once told.
"Goodness had nothing to do with it,"
she replied.

"Whether you think that you can, or that you can't, you're usually right."
Henry Ford

"There is nothing either good or bad,
but thinking makes it so."
Shakespeare, *Hamlet*

"As a rule, there is no surer way to the dislike
of men than to behave well where they have
behaved badly."
**Lew Wallace, US lawyer and Union general
in the American Civil War**

"Three things in life are important: the first is
to be kind; the second is to be kind; and the
third is to be kind."
Henry James

"If I had to live my life all over again, I'd do it
exactly the same – only I wouldn't read
Beowulf."
Woody Allen

"Everything looks
better after lunch."

Winston Churchill

Staying young

I once asked **Joan Collins** for the secrets of her success, says Gyles Brandreth. "How many do you want?" she replied, not batting an eyelid. "Five," I replied, ambitiously. She nodded, "narrowing her eyes", and began. "One, energy. Mine is God-given. My mother used to call me Miss Perpetual Motion because I never kept still. Two, exercise. Use it or lose it. That's true of everything. If you stop talking for a week, your tongue would atrophy.

Three, optimism. Cultivate it. Do you know the story of the twins who went into the shed full of horseshit? The first boy said, 'Ugh, this place smells terrible.' The second boy said, 'Mmm, horse shit... There must be a pony here somewhere.' Four, work, work, work. If you want to do something,

do it for yourself. Nobody ain't going to do it for you. Five, live for today. Remember yesterday is history, tomorrow is a mystery, today is a gift. That's why it's called the present." Her secrets have served her well: she turned 90 [in May 2023]. It's hard to believe, "even when you look very closely – and I have".

Joan has rattled through four husbands and a "casting directory" of A-List lovers – James Dean, Terence Stamp, and Ryan O'Neill, to name a few. None of them lasted: "You're a f***ing bore," one of them told her, "And you're a boring f***," replied Joan. But so far, her fifth husband Percy Gibson has survived. Handsome, funny and 31 years her junior – 21 years together and you can see it "clearly works".
The Oldie

~~~~~~~~~~

John D Rockefeller lived to 97. His doctor once revealed his simple secrets: "First, he avoids all worry. Second, he takes plenty of exercise in the open air. Third, he gets up from the table a little hungry."

Social life

"You must come again when you have less time."
**Painter Walter Sickert
to a departing guest**

"No one really listens to anyone else, and if you try it for a while you'll see why."
**American journalist
Mignon McLaughlin**

"There is no such thing as conversation. There are intersecting monologues, that is all."
Rebecca West

"If you haven't got anything nice to say come and sit next to me."
American socialite
Alice Roosevelt Longworth

"The first duty of a man is to speak; that is his chief business in the world; and talk, which is the harmonious speech of two or more, is by far the most accessible of our pleasures."
Robert Louis Stevenson

"Hear no evil, speak no evil, and you won't be invited to cocktail parties."
Oscar Wilde

> "Blessed is the man who,
> having nothing to say,
> abstains from giving us
> wordy evidence of the fact."
> **George Eliot**

~~~~~~~~~~~~~~~~~~~~~

Three might be a crowd, but when it comes to having an "enjoyable chat", says Oxford professor **Robin Dunbar**, four's the magic number. Studies have shown that when a fifth person joins in, the conversation splinters into two groups within about 20 seconds – or turns into a lecture with one person holding court.

This is why, for example, SAS patrols and surgical teams work best in groups of no more than four. And it's something William Shakespeare clearly recognised: his plays rarely have more than four significant characters speaking in any one scene. The playwright "instinctively understood the mentalising capacities" of a theatre audience – he didn't want them "overloaded" by too much on-stage action.

"Some cause happiness wherever they go; others whenever they go."
Oscar Wilde

"The aristocracy and the working classes will always unite against the middle classes in their love of sport and immorality."
Randolph Churchill

"It would have been splendid... if the wine had been as cold as the soup, the beef as rare as the service, the brandy as old as the fish, and the maid as willing as the duchess."
Winston Churchill on a dinner

"At my school we were taught that silence was the unbearable riposte."
Sir Alec Douglas-Home
British PM 1963-1964

HOW TO

SUCCEED IN

BUSINESS

"When you have exhausted all possibilities, remember this – you haven't."

Thomas Edison

"Doubt kills more dreams than
failure ever will."
American poet Suzy Kassem

"Talent sets the floor,
character sets the ceiling."
Bill Belichick
American football coach

"Be kind to everyone on the way up;
you'll meet the same people
on the way down."
Wilson Mizner
American playwright

"In any successful enterprise there
must be an uneven number of directors
and three is too many."
Founder of Fiat
Giovanni Agnelli

"A good leader is someone who takes a little more than his share of the blame and a little less than his share of the credit."
American author John C Maxwell

"The secret of power is the knowledge that others are more cowardly than you are."
German writer Ludwig Börne

"Concentration comes out of a combination of confidence and hunger."
Arnold Palmer

"The difference between successful people and very successful people is that very successful people say no to almost everything."
Warren Buffett

Faking it

Boris Johnson has always been a "skilled deceiver", says columnist **Matthew Syed**. In his book *Chums*, Simon Kuper tells of a formative moment at Balliol College, Oxford, when "good old Boris" was caught copying a translation straight out of a textbook. "I've been so busy," he told his tutor apologetically, "I just didn't have time to put in the mistakes." One is reminded of Evelyn Waugh's observation in *Brideshead Revisited*: "Those that have charm don't really need brains."
The Sunday Times

"All men are mad who devote themselves to the pursuit of power when they can be fishing or painting pictures, or sitting in the sun."

Historian AJP Taylor

"Forgive your enemies, but never forget
their names."
John F Kennedy

"Give people the chance to say 'no' to
you. If they say it enough, they will feel
beholden to you to come back with a
'yes' by way of compensation."
Hilary Rubin in *The Princessa*

"Genius is the infinite capacity
to take pains."
Journalist Victor Lewis-Smith

"The most difficult thing is the decision to act; the rest is merely tenacity."
Amelia Earhart, the first woman to fly solo across the Atlantic

"If you're going to do something, go start. Life's simpler than we sometimes can admit."
Robert De Niro

"A leader should be light-hearted and full of hope, by means of his facial expression, his words and his dress."
Marshal Montecuccoli, 17th-century Italian-born soldier and strategist

"Vulnerability is the condition of all achievement."
British literary critic Terry Eagleton

"Progress isn't made by early risers. It's made by lazy men trying to find easier ways to do something."
Robert Heinlein

"You don't get what you deserve. You get what you negotiate."
Boxing promoter Don King

"Most successes are unhappy. That's why they are successes – they have to reassure themselves by achieving something that the world will notice."
Agatha Christie

"The secret of life is honesty and fair dealing. If you can fake that, you've got it made."
Groucho Marx

"Men must be either pampered or crushed, because they can get revenge for small injuries but not for grievous ones."
Italian diplomat Niccolo Machiavelli

The importance of luck

"Lucky people are skilled at creating and noticing chance opportunities; make lucky decisions by listening to their intuition; create self-fulfilling prophecies via positive expectations; and adopt a resilient attitude that transforms bad luck into good."
Professor Richard Wiseman, author of *The Luck Factor*

"You never know what worse luck your bad luck has saved you from."
Cormac McCarthy

"We must believe in luck, for how else can we explain the success of those we don't like?"
French poet Jean Cocteau

THE
SECRET
OF
HAPPINESS

"We don't laugh because we're happy,
we're happy because we laugh."
**American philosopher
William James**

"To be without some of the things you
want is an indispensable part of
happiness."
Bertrand Russell

"What is happiness? It depends on two
assets, which fortunately I have. They
are good health and a short memory."
Ingrid Bergman

"The days that make us happy
make us wise."
John Masefield

"Hope is itself a species of happiness,
and, perhaps, the chief happiness which
this world affords."
Samuel Johnson

"Puritanism... the haunting fear that
someone, somewhere,
may be happy."
HL Mencken

"Everyone wants to live on the peak of the mountain, without knowing that the real happiness is in how it is scaled."
Gabriel García Márquez

"One is never as unhappy as one thinks, nor as happy as one hopes."
François de La Rochefoucauld

"To be happy, we must not be too concerned with others."
Albert Camus

"Sister Helen Loder was cycling through her parish when a boy shouted at her: 'F****** nun'. She dismounted from her bicycle and said: 'One or the other, but I can't be both.'"
Quoted by AN Wilson in the Evening Standard

"Happiness is not something you experience, it's something you remember."
American concert pianist Oscar Levant

"Happiness is an imaginary condition, formerly attributed by the living to the dead, now, usually attributed by adults to children, and by children to adults."
Psychiatrist Thomas Szasz

"Very happy people invariably like themselves."
Journalist Graham Turner

"If one can't be happy one must be amused, don't you agree?"
Nancy Mitford

"Happiness is having a large, loving,
caring, close-knit family
in another city."
Comedian George Burns

"I never lose sight of the fact that just
being is fun."
Katharine Hepburn

"Gloom is part of being British...
Depressing films and novels are
routinely considered more serious and
more worthy of attention. Happiness,
by contrast, seems insipid and trivial."
**Journalist and author
Marcus Berkmann**

"Thank heavens, the sun
has gone in and I don't
have to go out
and enjoy it."

Logan Pearsall Smith

"When I'm good, I'm very good, but when I'm bad, I'm better."
Mae West

"A lifetime of happiness? No man could bear it."
George Bernard Shaw

"If ignorance is bliss, this boy is in for a life of undiluted happiness."
School report quoted in a letter to The Times

"The happiest part of a man's life is what he passes lying awake in bed in the morning."
Samuel Johnson

"One of the secrets of a happy life is continuous small treats."
Iris Murdoch

Optimists and pessimists

"The nice part about being a pessimist is that you are constantly being either proven right or pleasantly surprised."
American columnist George Will

"A pessimist is a man who looks both ways before crossing a one-way street."
Canadian writer Laurence Peter

"Both optimists and pessimists contribute to society. The optimist invents the aeroplane, the pessimist the parachute."
George Bernard Shaw

Secrets

"A secret is something that is only repeated to one person at a time."
Writer and editor Robert McCrum

"He that has a secret should not only hide it, but hide that he has it to hide."
Thomas Carlyle

"A lot of secrets are quite hard to remember once you have heard them."
Charles Moore

OTHER
PEOPLE

"You can tell more about a person by what he says about others than you can by what others say about him."
Audrey Hepburn

"We only confess our little faults to persuade people that we have no large ones."
François de La Rochefoucauld

"Sometimes one likes foolish people for their folly better than wise people for their wisdom."
Elizabeth Gaskell

"What you say about somebody else, anybody else, reveals you."
US novelist and playwright
James Baldwin

"Few things can console us faster than hearing the misfortunes of others."
British author Alain de Botton

"Other people, as we get to know them,
are like strips of metal dipped in acid:
they gradually lose their good qualities –
and their defects too, at times."
Marcel Proust

"Whenever a friend succeeds, a little
something in me dies."
Gore Vidal

"Usually when one weeps one weeps for
oneself. That's the terrible truth."
Clive James

"One must not be a name-dropper, as Her
Majesty remarked to me yesterday."
Tory MP Norman St John-Stevas

Celebrities

"There are two kinds of great men, the little great men, who make all those around them feel little, and the great great men, who make all those around them feel great."
GK Chesterton

"When I left the dining room after sitting next to Mr Gladstone, I thought he was the cleverest man in England. But after sitting next to Mr Disraeli, I thought I was the cleverest woman in England."
Unknown but sometimes attributed to Jenny Jerome, Winston Churchill's mother.

"The nice thing about being a celebrity is that when you bore people, they think it's their fault."
Henry Kissinger

"Malibu is the only place in the world where you can lie on the sand and look at the stars – or vice versa."
Joan Rivers

"A celebrity is a person who works hard all his life to become known, then wears dark glasses to avoid being recognised."
American comedian Fred Allen

"Very often the most intolerant and narrow-minded people are the ones who congratulate themselves on their tolerance and open-mindedness."
Christopher Hitchens

"Most people are other people. Their thoughts are someone else's opinions, their life a mimicry, their passions a quotation."
Oscar Wilde

"One of the horribly character-forming things about life is that praise is least forthcoming from the people who know us best, and love us most."
Craig Brown

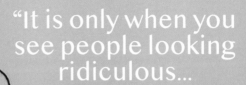

"It is only when you see people looking ridiculous...

...that you realise just how much you love them."

Agatha Christie

Lawyers

"A lawyer is a person who writes a 10,000-word document and calls it a brief."
Franz Kafka

"A good lawyer knows the law; an excellent lawyer knows the judge."
Legal aphorism

"I run my office on the fees I charge clients whom I advise not to sue for libel. And I run my Rolls-Royce on the fees I receive from clients who ignore my advice."
A libel lawyer talking to Victor Lewis-Smith

"A jury consists of 12 persons chosen to decide who has the better lawyer."
Robert Frost

"A bad lawyer is one who can make a case stretch on for ages. A good one can make it go on even longer."
Victoria Dowd (a lawyer)

The Old Bailey judge who sentenced the Kray twins to life in 1969 later said they'd told the truth only twice in the whole trial, "once when Reggie called a barrister a 'fat slob', and once when Ronnie said the judge was biased".
The Spectator

"The heart of another is a dark forest,
always, no matter how close it has been
to one's own."
Novelist Willa Cather

"You will become way less concerned
what other people think of you when you
realise how seldom they do."
**American writer
David Foster Wallace**

"Never speak ill of yourself. Your friends
will say enough on that subject."
Charles-Maurice de Talleyrand

"Our enemies come nearer the truth in
the opinions they form of us than we do
in our opinion of ourselves."
François de La Rochefoucauld

"The life of a person is not what
happened, but what he remembers
and how he remembers it."
Gabriel García Márquez

"Shyness is just egoism
out of its depth."
Actress Penelope Keith

"We never know the whole man, though
sometimes, in quick flashes,
we know the true man."
Agatha Christie

"It is shocking to discover how much ill-will and envy of the successful bubbles beneath the surface."
PD James on her critics

"Anyone going slower than you is an idiot and anyone going faster than you is a maniac."
Comedian Jerry Seinfeld on drivers

"Union leaders are remarkably even-tempered men – always angry."
Max Hastings

"Kindness is in our power, fondness is not."
Dr Johnson

"At 20, we worry about what others think of us; at 40, we don't care what they think of us; at 60, we discover they haven't been thinking of us at all."
Bob Hope

"Whatever you may be sure of, be sure of this: that you are dreadfully like other people."
US poet and critic
James Russell Lowell

"Imagining what it is like to be someone other than yourself is at the core of our humanity. It is the essence of compassion, and the beginning of morality."
Ian McEwan

Royalty

"In times when nothing stood
but worsened, or grew strange,
there was one constant good:
she did not change."
Philip Larkin on Queen Elizabeth II

~~~~~~~~~

The Queen was never much of a
football fan, says former FA chairman
David Triesman. "There are no horses,"
he says, "and, try as we might, we could
never find a way of involving horses in
football." He did once get the Queen to
a match at Wembley, which she seemed
to enjoy. Afterwards, Triesman asked
who she thought had played best. "The
band of the Scots Guards," she replied.

~~~~~~~~~

"The monarchy allows us to take a
holiday from reason; and on that
holiday we do no harm."
Martin Amis

"Power has little majesty in the British system. Prime ministers reside in an apartment over their office. People are rude to them all the time... Meanwhile, the person who gets the palaces, the bowing and scraping, the bands and the guards, gets nothing else."
US commentator David Frum on Britain's constitutional monarchy

"Where men are forbidden to honour a king they honour millionaires, athletes, or film stars instead: even famous prostitutes or gangsters. For spiritual nature, like bodily nature, will be served; deny it food and it will gobble poison."
CS Lewis

"Hell is other people at breakfast."
Anonymous variant of the original saying by Jean-Paul Sartre

"Among those whom I like or admire, I can find no common denominator, but among those whom I love, I can: all of them make me laugh."
WH Auden

"Charm is the ability to be truly interested in other people."
American photographer Richard Avedon

"There's no limit to what a man might accomplish if he doesn't mind who takes the credit."
Ronald Reagan

Friendship

Shortly after they campaigned together for Bob Dole in the 1996 US election, **George HW Bush** sent a note to his fellow former president Gerald Ford. "I hope you don't think this letter is odd and strange," it read. "I write simply to say I am very proud to be your friend. This friendship matters a lot to me – it really does. As you and I drove across that Ohio countryside last week, it hit me like a ton of bricks, that too often we fail to tell our friends that we really care about them and are grateful to them."

Solitude

The novelist **Ian McEwan** says he regrets "the passing of what I regard as one of the great luxuries of civilisation: solitude. I think those snatched moments – the 20 minutes when you're waiting at the luggage carousel – you used to have nothing to do but go into your thoughts." Now we all take out our phones – and perhaps we "don't have so rich an inner life". If you get in the habit of solitude – an entirely different thing from loneliness – you can "treat your mind as a garden and walk around it and I think generally it leads to more happiness".

Interview with the *Today* programme

The young

"I want my children to have all the things I couldn't afford. Then I want to move in with them."
American comedian Phyllis Diller

"Children begin by loving their parents; as they grow older they judge them; sometimes they forgive them."
Oscar Wilde

"There's a whole Twitter generation of people who hang around waiting to be offended. They wouldn't have won the war, would they?"
Robbie Coltrane

"A school report that perfectly summed up my daughter's personality read: 'Kate is the life and soul of the party; unfortunately we are not having a party.'"
Letter to The Daily Telegraph

"A happy childhood has spoiled many a promising life."
Canadian author Robertson Davies

"If there's one thing I hate more than the Welsh it's the young. I hate young people with a passion. I wish them all ill. People under the age of 40 don't see anything. Even if they do, they don't really know what they are seeing."
TV dramatist Dennis Potter

"Your youth evaporates in your early forties when you look in the mirror. And then it becomes a full-time job pretending you're not going to die, and then you accept that you'll die. Then in your fifties everything is very thin. And then suddenly you've got this huge new territory inside you, which is the past, which wasn't there before."
Martin Amis

Growing old

"An individual human existence should be like a river: small at first, narrowly contained within its banks, and rushing passionately past rocks and over waterfalls. Gradually the river grows wider, the banks recede, the waters flow more quietly, and in the end, without any visible break, they become merged in the sea, and painlessly lose their individual being."
Bertrand Russell in
How to Grow Old

"No pleasure is worth giving up for the sake of two more years in a geriatric home at Weston-Super-Mare."
Kingsley Amis

Passing on

On 6th February 1952, King George VI died in his sleep after a day of shooting at Sandringham. "I hope you will arrange something like that for me," **Winston Churchill** later told his doctor. "But don't do it till I tell you."

"When I die, I want to go peacefully like my grandfather did – in his sleep. Not yelling and screaming like the passengers in his car."
Comedian Bob Monkhouse

An apology sent out by barbecue maker Weber [in January 2022]:
"In today's email we highlighted a grilled meatloaf recipe. At the time we shared this recipe with you, we were not aware of the unfortunate passing of American singer and actor Mr Marvin Lee Aday, also known as Meat Loaf."

Posterity

Lives of great men remind us.
We can make our lives sublime
And departing leave behind us
Footprints on the sands of time.
Longfellow, from *A Psalm of Life* (1838)

Egypt's might is tumbled down
Down a-down the deeps of thought;
Greece is fallen and Troy town,
Glorious Rome hath lost her crown,
Venice' pride is nought.

But the dreams their children dreamed
Fleeting, unsubstantial, vain,
Shadowy as the shadows seemed,
Airy nothing, as they deemed,
These remain.
Elizabeth Coleridge, *Egypt's Might is Tumbled Down* (1907)

Enough, if something from our hands have power
To live, and act, and serve the future hour;
And if, as toward the silent tomb we go,
Through love, through hope, and faith's
transcendent dower,
We feel that we are greater than we know.
**Wordsworth, *Sonnets from the River Duddon:
After-Thought* (1820)**

To sail beyond the sunset, and the baths
Of all the western stars, until I die.
It may be that the gulfs will wash us down:
It may be we shall touch the Happy Isles,
And see the great Achilles, whom we knew.
Tho' much is taken, much abides; and tho'
We are not now that strength which in old days
Moved earth and heaven, that which we are, we
are; One equal temper of heroic hearts,
Made weak by time and fate, but strong in will
To strive, to seek, to find, and not to yield.
Tennyson, from *Ulysses* (1833)

BRITAIN
AND ITS
NEIGHBOURS

"The insularity of the English,
their refusal to take foreigners
seriously, is a folly that has to be
paid for very heavily
from time to time."
George Orwell

"Immigration is the sincerest form of flattery."
American talk show host Jack Parr

"The British will let you get away with almost anything if you make them laugh."
William Waldegrave

"The comfortably off ought always to bear in mind GK Chesterton's remark that the agreeable character of English life 'does not rest on the kindness of the rich to the poor. It rests on the perennial and unfailing kindness of the poor to the rich.'"
Journalist and author Ferdinand Mount

"Here is a country that fought and won a noble war, dismantled a mighty empire in a generally benign and enlightened way, created a far-seeing welfare state – in short, did nearly everything right – and then spent the rest of the century looking on itself as a chronic failure. The fact is that this is still the best place in the world for most things – to post a letter, go for a walk, watch television, buy a book, venture out for a drink, go to a museum, use the bank, get lost, seek help, or stand on a hillside and take in a view."

Bill Bryson, from
***Notes on a Small Island* (1995)**

"Curse... the blasted, jelly-boned swines, the snivelling, dribbling, dithering, palsied, pulse-less lot that make up England today. God, how I hate them! Why, why, why was I born an Englishman?"
DH Lawrence in a letter to Edward Garnett (1912)

"Europe was set up by clever, Catholic, left-wing, French bureaucrats. Most Brits have a problem with at least three of those five."
Historian Peter Hennessy

"I've had it with these dopey little countries and all their poky borders. You can't swing a cat without sending it through customs."
PJ O'Rourke on Europe

"One could hardly think of a worse name than the Euro. Two-syllable words ending with 'o' do not generally inspire confidence – weirdo, psycho, Rambo, porno, pseudo, gringo and bingo."
Journalist and author
Quentin Crewe

"When God created France He found it so perfect that, to comfort those who couldn't live there, He invented the French."
Old saying

"The English fondness for France is normally a sort of neutron love: take away the people and leave the buildings standing."
Anthony Lane in The New Yorker

"There has been a change in the national character – a reduction in conscience and self-control."
Professor Christie Davies
in *The Loss of Virtue* (1995)

"The French, unlike – and this cannot be said often enough, the Germans – hate the English. They hate us because in war we have never been defeated. While they, since the battle of Leipzig in 1813, have never been victorious."
MP and diarist Alan Clarke

"Who could dislike a man who, when told he'd been voted the 'most popular German', replied that he knew it was a very short list?"
Journalist Carol Midgley on Boris Becker

"Only Napoleon did more than I have done. But I am definitely taller."
Silvio Berlusconi

"I take care only to travel on Italian ships; in the event of disaster, there's none of that nonsense about women and children first."
Noël Coward

Russia

"I asked Boris Yeltsin to tell me briefly
what the situation in Russia was like.
'Good,' he said. I asked for a longer
version. 'Not good,' he replied."
John Major

Australia

"To live in Australia permanently is
rather like going to a party and dancing
all night with one's mother."
**Barry Humphries on why
he lived in England**

America

"Wherever there's injustice, oppression and suffering, America will show up six months late and bomb the country next to where it's happening."
PJ O'Rourke

"America is the only nation in history which miraculously has gone directly from barbarism to degeneration without the usual interval of civilisation."
French statesman Georges Clemenceau

"War is God's way of teaching Americans geography."
Short story writer Ambrose Bierce

"Each American embassy comes with two permanent features – a giant anti-American demonstration and a giant line for American visas."
PJ O'Rourke

"I dislike America and on the whole, though there are many exceptions to this, I dislike Americans. I find them as I find the English abroad: noisy and exceptionally ignorant about the world."
Graham Greene

"To the comment: 'You'll have the vote of every thinking American!' **Adlai Stevenson** replied: 'That's not enough, I need a majority.'"

"On some great and glorious day, the plain folks of the land will reach their heart's desire at last, and the White House will be adorned with a moron."
Essayist and critic HL Mencken

"Be nice to America – or we'll bring you democracy."
US bumper sticker after the invasion of Iraq

LOVE
ETC.

"When we let romance go, we change the sky for the ceiling."
English novelist George Meredith

"Absence diminishes mediocre passions and increases great ones, as the wind extinguishes candles and fans fires."
François de La Rochefoucauld

"I believe that sex is one of the most beautiful, natural, wholesome things that money can buy."
American comedian Steve Martin

"They say the definition of ambivalence is watching your mother-in-law drive over a cliff in your new Cadillac."
Playwright David Mamet

"Mama told me, be a maid in the living room, a cook in the kitchen and a mistress in the bedroom. But I hire someone to be a maid and someone to cook so I can take care of the rest."
Jerry Hall

"Love conquers all things except poverty and toothache."
Mae West

"There are a number of mechanical devices which increase sexual arousal, particularly in women. Chief among these is the Mercedes-Benz 380SL convertible."
PJ O'Rourke

"Everyone lies about sex. People lie during sex. If it weren't for lies, there'd be no sex."
Jerry Seinfeld

"Men want to be a woman's first love – women like to be a man's last romance."
Oscar Wilde

"Over a decade or so, the rhythm of most couples' sex lives goes from tri-weekly to try weekly to try weakly."
Victor Lewis-Smith

"You know 'that look' women get when they want sex? Me neither."
Steve Martin

"A man desires a woman, but a woman desires the desire of a man."
Madame de Staël

"We had a lot in common. I loved him and he loved him."
**Actress Shelley Winters
on her ex-husband**

"Sex is totally ludicrous to everybody except the participants."
**Playwright and screenwriter
Alan Plater**

"A kiss is an application on the top floor for a job in the basement."
Artwork at Spectrum Art Exhibition

"All you need is love. But a little chocolate now and then doesn't hurt."

Cartoonist Charles Schulz

Marriage

"I am a marvellous housekeeper. Every time I leave a man, I keep his house."
Zsa Zsa Gabor

"Never feel remorse for what you have thought about your wife; she has thought much worse things about you."
French biologist Jean Rostand

"My wife and I were happy for 20 years. Then we met."
American comedian Rodney Dangerfield

"My first wife drove me to drink. It's the only thing I'm indebted to her for."
WC Fields

"The critical period in matrimony is breakfast time."
Poet and satirist AP Herbert

"I don't think I'll get married again. I'll just find a woman I don't like and give her a house."
American writer Lewis Grizzard

"What do you mean how many husbands have I had? You mean apart from my own?"
Zsa Zsa Gabor

"Bigamy is having one wife too many. Monogamy is the same".
Oscar Wilde

"A marriage is always made up of two people who are prepared to swear that only the other one snores."
Terry Pratchett

"Like everything which is not the involuntary result of fleeting emotion but the creation of time and will, any marriage, happy or unhappy, is infinitely more interesting than any romance, however passionate."
WH Auden

"It doesn't matter much whom you marry because it always turns out to be someone else."
Old adage

"I still miss my husband, but my aim is improving."
Old joke

Men and women

"It's better to be looked over than overlooked."
Mae West

"An archaeologist is the best husband any woman can have: the older she gets, the more interested he is in her."
Agatha Christie

"Women dress alike all over the world. They dress to be annoying to other women."
**Italian fashion designer
Elsa Schiaparelli**

"A woman will always sacrifice herself, if you give her the opportunity. It is her favourite form of self-indulgence."
W Somerset Maugham

"What is the only thing that men and women have in common? I'll tell you. They both hate women."
Arabella Weir

"The male is a domestic animal who, if treated with firmness and kindness, can be trained to do most things."
Jilly Cooper

"Women are programmed to love completely and men are programmed to spread it around. We are fools to think it's any different."
Beryl Bainbridge

"A lasting relationship with a woman is possible only if you're a business failure."
J Paul Getty

"Love is the delusion that one woman differs from another."
HL Mencken

"The trouble with some women is that they get all excited about nothing – and then marry him."
Cher

To The Sunday Times

Decca Aitkenhead's article ("The real problem with men? They're rubbish at asking questions") rang so true. I have recently spent time with five men for various reasons. I now know all about them and their families. Not one has asked anything about me.

Yesterday a man who has been a sailing companion for six weeks tried to explain an offence of fraud to me. He has no clue that I am a criminal lawyer. He has never asked. Yet all of them believe we get on well. Not one has noticed that I am the one making conversation all the time.

Sarah Rogers, London

———————

I'll love you, dear, I'll love you,
Till China and Africa meet,
Till the river jumps over the mountain,
And the salmon sing in the street.

I'll love you till the oceans
Are folded and hung out to dry
And the seven seas go squawking,
Like geese about the sky.

WH Auden

So, we'll go no more a roving
So late into the night,
Though the heart be still as loving,
And the moon be still as bright.
Lord Byron

By the time you swear you're his,
Shivering and sighing.
And he vows his passion is,
Infinite, undying.
Lady make note of this –
One of you is lying.
Dorothy Parker

"Roddy Llewellyn told a story about a man going into the home of two spinsters to view a Ming vase and seeing a French letter lying on the piano stool. The old lady explained: 'We found it lying on the grass on the common and it said Place on organ to avoid infection and we haven't got an organ so we put it on the piano and you know we've neither of us had any colds this year!'"
From Gyles Brandreth's diaries

"Shoes don't stretch and men don't change."

American country singer Amy Dalley

MONEY

"Las Vegas is the only place I know
where money really talks – it says,
'Goodbye'."
Frank Sinatra

"There are two times in a man's life when he should not speculate: when he can't afford it and when he can."
Mark Twain

"He was gifted with the sly, sharp instinct for self-preservation that passes for wisdom among the rich."
Evelyn Waugh in *Scoop*

"I'm living so far beyond my income that we might almost be said to be living apart."
American poet EE Cummings

"A bank is a place that will lend you money if you can prove that you don't need it."
Bob Hope

"Everyone is always in favour of general economy and particular expenditure."
Anthony Eden, British PM 1955-57

"Too many people spend money they don't have on things they don't want to impress people they don't like."
American humourist Will Rogers

"The world is not driven by greed. It's driven by envy."
Investor Charlie Munger

"I feel these days like a very large flamingo. No matter what way I turn, there is always a very large bill."
Irish novelist Joseph O'Connor

"The idea that money doesn't buy happiness is a lie put about by the rich, to stop the poor from killing them."
Michael Caine

"Money – the one thing that keeps us in touch with our children."
Gyles Brandreth

"There are three types of economist: those who can count and those who can't."
Eddie George

"Gentlemen prefer bonds."
American banker Andrew Mellon

"You can be young without money but you can't be old without it."
Tennessee Williams

"My problem lies in reconciling my gross habits with my net income."
Errol Flynn

"I'm tired of love; I'm still more tired of rhyme; but money gives me pleasure all the time."
Hilaire Belloc

"The factory of the future will have only two employees: a man and a dog. The man will be there to feed the dog. The dog will be there to keep the man from touching the equipment."
Management guru Warren Bennis

"All I ask is the chance to prove that money can't make me happy."

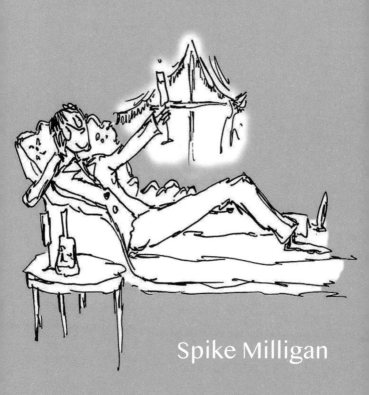

Spike Milligan

POLITICS

"The best argument against democracy is a five-minute conversation with the average voter."
Winston Churchill

"The business of progressives is to go on making mistakes. The business of conservatives is to prevent mistakes from being corrected."
GK Chesterton

"He has not a single redeeming defect."
**Benjamin Disraeli on
William Gladstone**

"God help the Tory party if the Tories ever get hold of it."
Matthew Parris

"The inherent vice of capitalism is the unequal sharing of blessings. The inherent virtue of socialism is the equal sharing of miseries."
Winston Churchill

"The trouble with socialism is that it takes too many evenings."
Oscar Wilde

"The difference between a welfare state and a totalitarian state is a matter of time."
Russian-American writer and philosopher Ayn Rand

"The trouble with socialism is socialism – but the trouble with capitalism is capitalists."
Austrian-American journalist Willi Schlamm

"Far better not."
Lord Hartington whenever any proposal or scheme was put to him

"One of life's abiding ironies is that people inclined towards ideological selfishness are often selflessly heroic towards individuals in need, whereas liberals talk a good game but don't always show up in a crisis."
Decca Aitkenhead

"Labour stands for envy and hope, the Conservatives for nostalgia and fear."
English novelist William Cooper

"The Republicans are the party that says government doesn't work, and then they get elected and prove it."
PJ O'Rourke

"Under capitalism, man exploits man, while under communism it's the other way round."
Old Czech joke

"Communism doesn't work because people like to own stuff."
American musician Frank Zappa

"Overseas aid is a transfer of money from poor people in rich countries to rich people in poor countries."
Hungarian-born British economist Peter Bauer

"I have orders to be awakened at any time in case of a national emergency, even if I'm in a cabinet meeting."
Ronald Reagan

"The poor object to being governed badly; the rich to being governed at all."
GK Chesterton

"Communism is the longest path from capitalism to capitalism."
Old Russian joke

BOOKS

"I think you will find that the sun is always shining in my books – a state of affairs which minutely lifts the spirit of the English reader."

Ian Fleming

"The great Russian novels of the 19th century arise from the failure of a class, whereas the English spring out of its success."
VS Pritchett

"Books say: she did this because. Life says: she did this. Books are where things are explained to you; life is where they aren't."
Julian Barnes

"They loved in triangles and lived in squares."
Dorothy Parker
on the Bloomsbury group

"Happy endings depend entirely on stopping the story before it's over."
Orson Welles

"The truth is that the greatness of
English literature for most of this
century resides not in adult novels but
in writing for children. I genuinely think
that Roald Dahl is a greater writer
than Martin Amis."
Columnist Melanie McDonagh

"Do I believe it? Do I care?
Will I go on caring?"
**Philip Larkin's three criteria
for a good novel**

"The purpose of art is washing the dust
of daily life off our souls."
Pablo Picasso

"The true aim of writing is to enable the
reader better to enjoy life, or better to
endure it."
Samuel Johnson

"Until one has some kind of professional relationship with books, one does not discover how bad the majority of them are."
George Orwell

"This is not a novel to be tossed aside lightly. It should be thrown with great force."
Dorothy Parker in a book review

"Childhood is the bank balance of the writer."
Graham Greene

"We make art from the quarrel with ourselves, mere rhetoric from the quarrel with others."
WB Yeats

"Some say life is the thing, but I prefer reading."

Logan Pearsall Smith

The art of writing

"How do I know what I think until I see
what I say?"
EM Forster

"All I can do is turn a phrase until it
catches the light."
Clive James

"It's like a strain on the eyesight. I find
that I have to know — even if I'm not
writing it — where my character's
sitting, what his movements are. It's
this focusing, even though it's not
focusing on the page, that strains my
eyes, as though I were watching
something too close."
Graham Greene

"I knew one thing about each of my
characters which I never told the
reader."
Arthur Ransome

"Every writer knows that the crucial part of his work is neither logical nor random, but the fruit of a mysterious process which we call, for want of a better word, 'inspiration'. The best jokes, the most tear-jerking moments, the intellectually satisfying twists simply come; they drift into the mind, amusing and moving the surprised author no less than his reader."
Writer Anthony Lejeune, in a letter to The Daily Telegraph

"I have made this letter longer than usual, only because I have not had the time to make it shorter."
Mathematician Blaise Pascal

"Make 'em cry, make 'em laugh, make 'em wait."
Wilkie Collins

"Don't tell me the moon is shining. Show me the glint of light on broken glass."
Anton Chekhov

Modern novels

"Novels today are all about women being sad in Fulham."
Kingsley Amis

Novelists struggle nowadays, says **Ferdinand Mount** (writing in the TLS), because of the disappearance of the old imperial values of restraint and self-sacrifice – what he calls *romanitas*.

"Is it possible that writers actually needed romanitas as a great flawed project to grate against, as something that generated tragedies and ironies that were worth dealing with, and that without romanitas life seems to have less to it?"

Shakespeare

"My own view is that probably none of the plays were written by Shakespeare, but by someone of the same name."
Frank Johnson

"England has two books, the Bible and Shakespeare. England made Shakespeare, but the Bible made England."
Victor Hugo

"My mother's married my uncle, only weeks after my father's death. My father's ghost keeps telling me to kill my uncle, but I don't feel like it. Anyway, I've just killed my girlfriend's father. My girlfriend's gone and drowned herself. I think her brother is trying to kill me."
Frank Johnson, on how *Hamlet* might have summarised his problems to Oprah Winfrey

Jane Austen

> "Jane Austen is Mills and Boon written by a genius."
>
> **PD James**

> "How seldom readers seem to remark on all that contempt for the whole human scene that lies just under the surface."
>
> **Thornton Wilder**

Shaw

George Bernard Shaw: "I am enclosing two tickets to the first night of my new play. Bring a friend... if you have one."
Winston Churchill: "Cannot possibly attend first night, will attend second... if there is one."

DH Lawrence

From an anonymous review of Lady Chatterley's Lover *by the magazine Field and Stream*

This fictional account of the day-to-day life of an English gamekeeper contains many passages on pheasant raising, apprehension of poachers, ways to control vermin and other chores of the professional gamekeeper. Unfortunately, one is obliged to wade through many pages of extraneous material in order to discover these sidelights. In this reviewer's opinion this book cannot take the place of JR Miller's *Practical Gamekeeping*.

THE WORLD

AND

HOW WE

SEE IT

"As I looked out into the night sky,
across all those infinite stars, it
made me realise how
insignificant they are."
Peter Cook

"The real problem of humanity is that we have palaeolithic emotions, medieval institutions and godlike technology."
Biologist EO Wilson

"Mankind is facing a crossroads – one road leads to despair and utter hopelessness and the other to total extinction. Let us pray we have the wisdom to choose correctly."
Woody Allen

"In headaches and in worry vaguely life leaks away."
WH Auden

"By the time a man realises that his father was right, he has a son who thinks he's wrong."
Pianist Charles Wadsworth

"It is only shallow people who do not judge by appearances."
Oscar Wilde

"Life is easy to chronicle, but bewildering to practise."
EM Forster

"Progress might have been alright once, but it has gone on too long."
Ogden Nash

"I don't believe in astrology; I'm a Sagittarius and we're sceptical."
Arthur C Clarke

"Thinking is to humans as swimming is to cats; they can do it but they'd prefer not to."
Psychologist & Nobel Prize winner Daniel Kahneman

"Millions long for immortality, who don't know what to do with themselves on a rainy Sunday afternoon."
Novelist Susan Ertz

"Most of the trouble in the world is caused by people wanting to be important."
TS Eliot

"Paranoia means having all the facts."
William Burroughs

"The art of being wise is the art of knowing what to overlook."
William James

Cleopatra, who lived from 69-30BC, was closer in time to the launch of the iPhone (2007) than the construction of the Great Pyramid of Giza (around 2600BC).

"We know what we are, but know not what we may be."
Ophelia in Shakespeare's *Hamlet*

"A man can stand anything, except a succession of ordinary days."
Wolfgang von Goethe

"I like work. It fascinates me. I can sit and look at it for hours."
Jerome K Jerome

"The less you know the better you sleep."
Russian proverb

"Often it does seem a pity that Noah and his party did not miss the boat."
Mark Twain

"There is always a well-known solution to every human problem – neat, plausible and wrong."
American writer HL Mencken

"What we call progress is the exchange of one nuisance for another nuisance."
English doctor and writer Havelock Ellis

"It's better to be quotable than honest."
Tom Stoppard

"I'm sure the universe is full of intelligent life. It's just been too intelligent to come here."
Arthur C Clarke

Religion

"Reason is itself a matter of faith. It is an act of faith to assert that our thoughts have any relation to reality at all."
GK Chesterton

"The English are not a very spiritual people, so they invented cricket to give them some idea of eternity."
George Bernard Shaw

"If it turns out that there is a God, I don't think that he's evil. But the worst that you can say about him is that basically he's an under-achiever."
Woody Allen

"I don't want to miss out on heaven due to a technicality."
Elvis Presley on why he wore a cross,
a star of David and the Hebrew letter chai

"Oppression is what they do in the West. What they do in the Middle East is their 'culture'."
Robert Harris

"Atheism is a crutch for those who can't bear the reality of God."
Tom Stoppard

"I don't believe in God, but I miss him."
Julian Barnes

To The Times:
Last year I drove past a church in south London outside which was a sign proclaiming "God Loves Man" – to which someone had added the word "United".
N Jeremy Taylor, London

As a choir boy, **Gyles Brandreth** sometimes sang at London's Holy Trinity Brompton church. "I loved this job," he tells The Daily Telegraph. He would get half a crown for weddings and five shillings for funerals, and therefore remembers "really wanting more funerals". The choir boys would kneel down, survey the congregation and agree on who was the oldest-looking member. "And we would pray to God to kill them." Sooner or later, their prayers would be answered. "I loved the fact that God was on the side of the entrepreneur."

"A professor is one who talks in someone else's sleep."
WH Auden

"Some ideas are so preposterous that only an intellectual could believe in them."
George Orwell

"Worry is interest paid on trouble before it falls due."
Dean Inge

"My loathings are simple: stupidity, oppression, crime, cruelty, soft music."
Vladimir Nabokov

"There are moments when everything turns out right. Don't be frightened: they pass."
French author Jules Renard

"All of humanity's problems stem from man's inability to sit quietly in a room alone."
Blaise Pascal

"Times are bad. Children no longer obey their parents and everyone is writing a book."
Cicero

"Hope is the feeling we have that the feeling we have is not permanent."
Mignon McLaughlin

"Nothing matters very much, and few things matter at all."
Arthur Balfour
British PM 1902-05

"The great thing to remember is that things aren't as bad as they were in the 14th century."
Tom Holland

The last word

This is an excerpt from a letter written by Evelyn Waugh (while serving with a commando unit in south-west Scotland) to his wife Laura on 31st May 1942.

Darling

No. 3 Cmdo were very anxious to be chums with Lord Glasgow so they offered to blow up an old tree stump for him and he was very grateful and he said don't spoil the plantation of young trees near it because that is the apple of my eye and they said no of course not we can blow a tree down so that it falls on a sixpence and Lord Glasgow said goodness you are clever and he asked them all to luncheon for the great explosion. So Col. Durnford-Slater D.S.O. said to his subaltern, have you put enough explosive in the tree. Yes, sir, 75 lbs. Is that enough? Yes sir I worked it out by mathematics it is exactly right. Well better put a bit more. Very good sir.

And when Col. D. Slater D.S.O. had had his port he sent for the subaltern and said subaltern better put a bit more explosive in that tree. I don't want to disappoint

Lord Glasgow. Very good sir.

   Then they all went out to see the explosion and Col. D.S. D.S.O. said you will see that tree fall flat at just that angle where it will hurt no young trees and Lord Glasgow said goodness you are clever.

   So soon they lit the fuse and waited for the explosion and presently the tree, instead of falling quietly sideways, rose 50 feet into the air taking with it ½ acre of soil and the whole of the young plantation.

   And the subaltern said Sir I made a mistake, it should have been 7½ lbs not 75.

   Lord Glasgow was so upset he walked in dead silence back to his castle and when they came to the turn of the drive in sight of his castle what should they find but that every pane of glass in the building was broken.

   So Lord Glasgow gave a little cry & ran to hide his emotion in the lavatory and there when he pulled the plug the entire ceiling, loosened by the explosion, fell on his head.

   This is quite true.

E

THE
KNOWLEDGE

The Knowledge is a daily newsletter that makes news manageable. It takes just five minutes to read, bringing together the things that matter, along with a few that don't, from all the best news sources. As we like to say, read less, know more.

To sign up, head to
www.theknowledge.com

What our readers say:

"Reading The Knowledge is one of my daily highlights."

"I am writing to let you know how immensely I have enjoyed reading your newsletter. Seriously witty and just the right side of cleverly informative."

"The Knowledge is one of the few subscriptions I've retained and worth every minute of my day."